Guisborough

past and present

Pam Wilson

Publishing Details

First published in Great Britain in 2005 by
Westgate Publishing

British Library Cataloguing in Publication Data. A catalogue record for this book is available from the British Library

ISBN (10-digit) 1-905544-02-2
ISBN (13-digit) 978-1-905544-02-8

Edited and designed by Westgate Publishing, 13 Farndale Drive, Pine Hills, Guisborough, TS14 8JD

Email: info@westgate-publishing.co.uk

Internet: www.westgate-publishing.co.uk

Preface

Guisborough's popularity shows no sign of diminishing in the twenty-first century. New developments and revitalisation since the millennium demonstrate a continuing confidence in the area. And while it is easy to become sentimental about the things we have lost, the expanding residential estates bring new energy and wealth to the town and help maintain its momentum.

Change, if carefully managed, is what keeps a place alive; the problem is knowing what to keep and what to throw away.

In the nineteen-sixties much was thrown away. Probably the saddest loss was the Guisborough branch railway, together with its attractive station buildings and house. These, and a row of nearby cottages, were demolished in 1967 to make way for the Fountain Street car park and Health Centre.

From a business point of view the railway was losing money and could no longer be justified. It was underused and had fallen victim to other forms of transport such as motor cars and buses. But the planners had not foreseen the massive expansion of the town in later years, nor the problems with road transport. Consequently our modern-day journey to Middlesbrough centre takes significantly longer than the 20 minutes it took on the train. So much for progress.

As a reminder of those days we publish a series of photographs taken in February 1964, by Maurice Burns, on the day Guisborough Station finally closed to the public. This collection was exhibited in Guisborough Library in 2004 to mark the 40th anniversary of the closure. Other contributors, notably Mark Lloyd and Geoff Scurr, have generously provided additional photographs showing the railway at different points in its history—from the golden years of the early twentieth century to the demolitions of the nineteen-sixties. Together these photographs form the most comprehensive collection ever published.

Fortunately recent developments are more in sympathy with their surroundings and conservation now often takes the place of demolition. The architectural horrors of the sixties and seventies have given way to buildings which are much more attractive.

As an added bonus, several historic houses around the town have recently been restored by sensitive owners and builders using traditional materials. Things are finally beginning to improve.

In *Guisborough past and present*, Pam Wilson's third book on the Guisborough area, we celebrate some of these recent achievements as well as looking back nostalgically to the way things used to be. We may have a long way to go, but we are getting there. I hope you enjoy the journey.

Paul Smith (Editor)

Acknowledgements

The front cover is based on a watercolour painting by D Booth. The rear cover photograph of the Christmas lights in Westgate was taken by Paul Smith in December 2004.

Contributors

This book would not have been possible without the many people who have shared their memories of Guisborough or provided photographs. They have all contributed to a unique picture of life in Guisborough—both past and present. They are:

Ronnie Allen

Brian Barnes

David Boyes

John Brelstaff

Ian and Pat Brown

Mary Brown (deceased)

Maurice Burns

Barbara Camidge

Nick Carter

Barry Cleaver

Pauline Clements

Brian Collins

Janet Coulson

Fred Dadd

Hugh Davies

Ron Durrans

Dave Emms

Sidney England (deceased)

Mr I Harrington

Carole Harris

Hilary Riach

Freda Knaggs

David Lawrence

John Linton

Mark Lloyd

Barry Parvin

Pat's Barber Shop

Edmund Phillips

Don Robinson

Frank Russell

Geoff Scurr

Colin Smiley

John Storey

Ann Sunley

Teesside Archives

Rosemary Thomas

Mr W N Thompson

Dave Trigg

Dora Trigg

Roy Walton

Wilson Weatherhead

Margaret Wilson

Thank you!

Contents

Chapter 1

People and Places

Hutton girls at Pauline Inman's birthday party c1950. Back row left to right: Marta Woolley, -?-, -?-, Pam Wilson, Isobel Calvert. Middle row left to right: Dorothy Boston, Barbara Jeffels, Margaret Taylor, Jennifer Fulton, -?-. Front row left to right: Pat Wilson, Pauline Inman and Rosemary Woolley

Back row left to right: Margaret Cleaver, Jessie Inman, Christine Hill and Anne Devon. Middle row left to right: Pam Wilson, Barbara Gull, Ann Jeffels, Isobel Calvert, Marta Woolley and Hilary Jeffels. Front row left to right: Pat Brown, Pauline Inman, Barbara Jeffels, -?-, Carole Devon

Previous page: This was the Hutton Gate Sunday School in 1946—all three of them! Carole Devon, Pat Brown and Anne Devon met with the Rector, Basil Shaw, each Sunday for their class which was held in, of all places, the railway station waiting room on the Hutton Lane side of the platform. Later the Sunday School was taught by Margaret Cleaver and held in Stable House

Hutton Gate (left and below)

Hutton Gate children. Back left to right: Russell Dermont, Marta Woolley, Carole Devon, Pat Brown, Isobel Calvert, Margaret Taylor and Vernon Birch. Front left to right: Lorraine East, -?-, -?-, Pamela Marshall, Diana Wrigley, Barbara Jeffels, Jennifer Deadman and Pauline Inman

Well-disguised Hutton children, but still mostly recognisable. Back left to right: Hilary Jeffels, Pat Brown, Pamela Hill, -?-, Carole Devon. Middle row left to right: Marta Woolley, Pamela Marshall, Barbara Jeffels, Pauline Inman, Sheila Hill. Front left to right: Fay Hill, Jennifer Deadman and Lorraine East

Walker's Row

The houses in Walker's Row were tiny: one living room and a kitchen with cold tap and two bedrooms above. The back yards were shared, usually 3 or 4 houses to a yard, with outside toilets and coal houses. It is incredible how people managed when you consider that families were much larger then, often having upwards of six children.

Walker's Row, now demolished

Sidney England, who sadly passed away this year, had a remarkable memory and told many stories of Guisborough in the 'olden days'. He remembered the names of many of the people who lived in Walker's Row; with additions from Freda Knaggs

I will list them as they could be useful to anyone researching family history:

Lightwing, White, Wilson, Scaise, Gallagher, Thrower, Bird, Blowman, Kerr, Beeforth, Milburn, Blake, Trigg, Bowers, Fairburn, Bush, McLean, Watson, Spencer, Westacott, Heseltine, Gage, Buck, Woodhouse, Morley, Fields, England, Dewing, Knaggs, Pearey, Stephenson and Russell.

The Fire Station was at the bottom end of Walker's Row, towards Northgate and Union Street. Across the end of Walker's Row was a wall where now you walk onto Northgate. At the Redcar Road end was Elsie Watson's shop, after which, on Redcar Road itself opposite the Park Hotel, was a bakery shop, Smith's, and then behind Walker's Row was Auckland Street with Budd's excellent fish and chip shop and Kyme's general shop.

The street was well festooned whenever there was a celebration, and this is the Silver Jubilee of George V in 1935. Among the ladies standing on the pavement are Nancy Trigg and Mrs England

Karl 'Billy' Weatherhead outside the shop, decorated for the Silver Jubilee of George V in 1935

Turning right from Walker's Row onto Redcar Road brought you to Wilson and Weatherhead's shop on the next corner, always neat as a new pin with the goods emptied from the window each Monday morning in readiness for a thorough cleaning and a new display.

The photograph above shows the shop with its patriotic display of flags, and highly decorated, again in 1935 for the King's Jubilee, and the owner Karl Weatherhead. (I can imagine the number of people at the moment saying 'that's wrong!', but it is not. Mr Weatherhead was never known as anything other than 'Billy', but his name was actually Karl.)

In the display above, the window is full of Rowntrees gums, Rowntrees chocolates, Wills Gold Flake and Navy Cut tobacco.

On the left is Jill Smith, from the bakery shop, next is young Wilson Weatherhead then Mabel Bridges

Albion Terrace, 1937. The house in the background is where Miss Firth had a private girls' school. From left to right are Mabel Bridges, Wilson Weatherhead and Marjorie Collins

Sitting in the back yard of Weatherhead's shop are Wilson Weatherhead and his uncle, Tom Bridges

At the end of Albion Terrace stand two proud young owners of bicycles, Wilson Weatherhead and Frank Wilkinson. Across the road in the background can be seen Harrison's paint and decorating business on the left and Storey's Funeral Directors on the right

Redcar Road

This shop stood at the end of Walker's Row and was at one time run by a Carey family. It was remembered by Freda Knaggs as being Elsie Watson's shop and in more recent times was 'Gifts and Gadgets'

William (Bill) Storey began his business of Funeral Directors in 1926 in a workshop at the back of Bennison Street and moved from there to Redcar Road in 1932–4. This photograph shows him at the back of Redcar Road in 1960

John Storey began working for his father in 1945 and this photo shows John inside the workshop

Playing cricket on the 'Fair Field' before houses were built are Alan Pearson, Arthur Clements, Alan Ord and one other who I'm sure someone will be able to name? Taken by John Storey with his Box Brownie camera he has captured the Police Station very well

Taken in the Grammar School top field, this gives a different view of the school and the cricket pavilion

Back on Redcar Road, overlooking the Fair Field, stood the Park Hotel.

The former Park Hotel, 36 Redcar Road

Roy Walton, former resident and chef at the Park Hotel, remembers the golden years...

'My parents bought the Park Hotel in 1947, I believe it had traded for a couple of years before. It was opened for B & B, Morning Coffee, Lunches, Afternoon Teas, High Teas, and Dinner. There were seven letting rooms, residents' lounge and dining room seating 30 with an overflow in our private lounge for another 10 people.

Mother did the housekeeping, cooking, and washing with the help of Swiss girls that came to work and learn English for one year. They usually did the waitressing.

In 1951 when I was 15 I left school and went to work for my parents, training as a cook and all the other aspects of catering. I left in 1954 to join the RAF and they carried on for a couple more years before turning it into flats for a rental income as my father's health by this time had deteriorated. My father died in 1962 and mother stayed on for 20 years, and when her mobility deteriorated we sold the house to Mackinley Hyde Motors.

Guisborough was a comfort stop for coaches travelling south from Tyne and Wearside to Scarborough and Bridlington. Father used to go into the High Street and persuade coach drivers to go straight to the Park Hotel where tea and biscuits were available at 6 pence with toilet facilities at hand, keeping all passengers together, no stragglers. Parking two or three coaches at a time in Redcar Road was a little difficult.

As time went by we were known by more and more drivers and their companies who started to make advance bookings for lunches and High Teas, or sometimes an evening stop on their Mystery Tours which were very popular in those days. We had many regulars staying in the Hotel, both commercial travellers and holiday-makers.'

1876 plans for the interior of 36 Redcar Road

'Plans for Shop and two cottages, Redcar Road, owner Mr James Purdy' (Teesside Archives reference DC/GU 27A 199 dated 11.11.1876). The 1890 census records show that 'Pallister Wm., cabinet maker, &c.,' was the resident at the time

An end view of the Park Hotel in 2005

Roy Walton, former chef at the Park Hotel, features in the next photograph...

Members of the Congregational Chapel and Youth Club, c1952. Back row, left to right: Jimmy Thrower, Brian Walker, Beryl Ward, Stan Jackson, Maureen Blackett, Billy Booth, Bill Peacock, Gerard Crewe, Roy Walton, Wilson Weatherhead, Arthur Rowlands, Howard Smith, Joyce Ward. Middle row, left to right: Christina McIntyre, Pat Blake, Sheila Walker, Marian Boyes, Jennifer Arnott, Brenda Cleaver, Margaret Williams, Margaret Cleaver, Elaine Fawcett, Rosemary Nicholson, Maureen Milward. Front row, left to right: Mary Cleaver (the organist), Mrs Smith, -?-, David Smith, Mr Crewe, Mr Rowlands, Maureen Stamper, Mr Smith

In March 1954 the Guisborough Boys' Club were the winners of the Proctor Cup. The players, from the left at the back are Roy Dewing, Wilson Weatherhead, Brown, Knight and A Clements. In the front are Sam Waterson, Ron Mudd, Knaggs, John Collinson and John Smith

Back in town, at the junction of Hollymead Drive and Bolckow Street, Billy Young (left) and Arthur Claxton (right) stand proudly in front of the newly built Hollymead Filling Station (Fred Dadd collection)

Day Trips and Holidays

June 24 1938. Among this group of Guisborough children, on a visit to Patterdale in the Lake District, are Jean Nicholson and Dora Kidd

Gentlemen of the Quoit Club Domino School at Blackpool on a trip. Left to right are Bill Weatherhead, Mr Hauxwell snr, Laurie Brittain and Len Willerton

Members of the 'Congs' Youth Club about to leave Guisborough Station for a walking holiday on the Isle of Wight (1952). From left to right: Gerard Crewe, Stan Jackson, Howard Smith, Brenda Cleaver, Maureen Blackett, Wilson Weatherhead, David Smith, Kathleen Cleaver, and Mr Crewe the Minister of the Chapel

(left) This photograph shows the Guisborough Co-operative milkmen in Helmsley, on a well-earned day off, c1956.

At the back is the Co-op Dairy Manager, Henry Robinson.

In the centre, left to right are Bill (Giner) Naylor and Ernie Robinson the van roundsman.

At the front are John (Jack) Russell, Frank Russell and Bill Guite.

More Memories...

From left to right: Bill Boyes, Robert Boyes, Thomas Edward Boyes, John Boyes, Fred Boyes. All born at 81, Charltons Terrace near Guisborough. Their parents were Alfred Edward and Sarah Annie Boyes

Emma Hewling, Hannah Lewis and Syd Hewling, and Margaret Lewis in front. Mr Hewling was Custodian of the Priory for many years until he died while cutting the grass in 1952

Margaret Lewis in New Road, c1957. The car is a Humber Supersnipe, the company car of the Director of Lancashire Steel. Margaret's uncle was the chauffeur and when he drove to Guisborough on a visit it caused quite a stir of excitement

Margaret and David Lewis in New Road, c1951. On the right is the building that is now Wetherell's

Obviously too young for their own wedding these two children must have been ready for one of Guisborough's many carnivals

John William Boyes, nicknamed 'Old Notion', with his grandson Robert Fletcher who was born in 1927

A neighbourly chat taking place in New Road with Mrs Blackburn on the left and Hannah Lewis on the right

William Nicholson, whose family had the florist shop and nursery where Boyes is now situated, stands proudly in his allotment near his home in Thompson Street. The allotments were on the land now occupied by Stump Cross bungalows and houses, stretching to the other side of the beck

Harry Lewis in his RAF uniform with his sister Peggy and brother Jess, standing in front of windows that are securely taped to prevent flying glass in the event of a bomb blast (June 26 1940)

Mrs Liverseed (left) and Maxine Stainsby near the holding pens at the cattle mart in Union Street. The weekly mart was very busy with farmers travelling into Guisborough from many of the outlying villages

An exceptionally lifelike drawing of Scott Blowman and Alan (Sam) Dawson in the blacksmith shop at Newstead Farm, by W N Thompson (1977)

Brian Barnes outside the cottages in Aysdale Gate, with the disused mineshaft in the background

(above) Aysdale Gate, 1964. A young Brian Barnes plays in front of the cottages.

In the background is the brick shaft of the former Aysdale Gate ironstone mine, which operated in the eighteen-seventies.

The shaft was eventually reduced in height and capped in the early nineteen-seventies, giving residents a brief opportunity to get rid of their rubbish.

Legend has it that even an old caravan went down the shaft!

Dave Trigg in Westgate Park, c1964

The Registry Office for births, deaths and
marriages was originally in this house in Gill Street

Fine doors on the Redcar Road houses are a good
background for Kathleen Cleaver, Ron Durrans
and Brenda Cleaver in the nineteen-forties

Aysdale Gate, 1963. Clockwise from left are Michael Barnes, Pauline Barnes and Sandra Barnes

Aysdale Gate children in 1966. From left: Sandra Barnes, Heather Thorpe, Zane Thirwall, Pauline Barnes, Bernadette Thorpe, Michael Barnes, and friends

Back in Guisborough, at Johnson's Yard, one of several new developments around the town. These 'before and after' photographs show how this previously run-down area has been transformed (Paul Smith)

Inside Johnson's Yard before rebuilding started...

...and after its transformation (Paul Smith)

On the corner opposite Wetherell's a new house is being built...

...and it soon looks like it was always there (Paul Smith)

A very early photograph of Westgate House showing the balcony and adjoining building

Westgate House in 2005, sensitively restored and much improved in recent years (Paul Smith)

Another house on Westgate looking spectacular after recent restoration work (Paul Smith)

Holly House presents another fine example of sensitive refurbishment (Paul Smith)

The new fence at Sunnyfield House nears completion in September 2005 (Paul Smith)

*Great attention to period detail—the reinstatement of authentic
'Yorkshire' horizontal sliding sash windows (Paul Smith)*

*Guisborough Town Hall, a grand Georgian building, waits patiently
for its refurbishment (Paul Smith)*

The Chaloner Hospital during redevelopment into apartments, 2005 (Paul Smith)

Chaloner Hospital—during redevelopment...

...and after (Paul Smith)

Saved! The Council makes an inspired decision to sell Cemetery Lodge for residential use (Paul Smith)

The Proclamation of King Edward VII in 1901, in the Market Place. The buildings in the background are the National Provincial Bank of England Limited, on the right, and J W Frank, Chemist, on the left. The photographer's vantage point, well above the height of the crowd, was presumably achieved by his climbing up the Market Cross—not easy considering the weight of an early 20th-century camera!

A group of well-dressed cyclists outside The Ship preparing for a ride. The only person who can be identified is David Boon, the gentleman in the white jacket on the left (Dora Trigg)

A decorated Peacock lorry with a cargo of knights on Carnival day

Carnival day—the children's band entertains

Firemen standing beside their Fire Engine, including Sidney England, Harold Hoggarth, Jack Reid, Ronnie Watson, Peter Jeffels, Fred Pickthall, Divisional Officer Winter, and Bert Armstrong

Members of Guisborough Fire Brigade in the mid-twentieth-century. On the back row, left to right are: John England, Fred Pickthall, Sidney England, Jack Reid, Tilley, -?-. Middle row, left to right: -?-, Bert Armstrong, Fred Welford, -?-. Front row left to right: Byles, Howard Christian, Brian Lines, Peter Jeffels. As late as 1963 the fire alarm was still operated from the Telephone Exchange where, on receiving the alert of a fire, the telephonist rang the fire bell continuously until the first fireman to arrive at the fire station called the Exchange. The bell shrilled out and was heard all over town and the firemen, who had permanent jobs as well, immediately 'downed tools' wherever they were and ran or cycled or begged lifts, using any means possible to get to the fire engine

The shield states; 'Annual Station Efficiency Competition. Presented to the most efficient retained station in A Division.' Back left to right; Sidney England, Jack Reid, Tommy Bawden, Bob Wood, Jack Hirst, Atkinson, -?-.Front left to right; -?-, -?-, Corbrick, -?-, George Ramshaw

Firemen with the fire engine in the Council yard in Walker's Row, c1947. That was the year that Mr Sidney England joined the Fire Service. Back left to right: Tilley, -?-, Fred Welford the Sub Officer, Sidney England, Wilf Payne. Front left to right: Bob Wood, Tommy Bawden, Outhwaite, George Wood and Jack Reid

Dave Emms, aka The Barmy Barber

Dave Emms in his smart outfit when the theme for Chaloner Street was a Victorian night

Dave the Barmy Barber was always ready for a bit of fun, especially if it involved making money for charity, and he helped to start the Christmas late-night opening for shops in Chaloner Street. Since then it has escalated and now involves all the shops in the town centre, with prizes for the best window displays, a visit from Santa and his reindeer, carol singing round the Christmas tree by the local schoolchildren and lots more.

In about 1989 a money raising idea of Dave's was a Challenge Race, over the moors to the Cleveland Inn at Commondale which was to involve runners, cyclists and horses, and the charity that was to benefit was the Cervical Cancer Unit at South Cleveland Hospital. There

was much debate as to whether the police would allow the parade of nude Lady Godiva (yes, she wore a body stocking!) through the streets of Guisborough, but the group was in luck. The police Inspector was a lady, who was much in favour of the charity they had chosen, and so permission was gladly given. Some stretches of the course were more favourable to cyclists and runners, which levelled out the chances a little, but the race was eventually won by the horses.

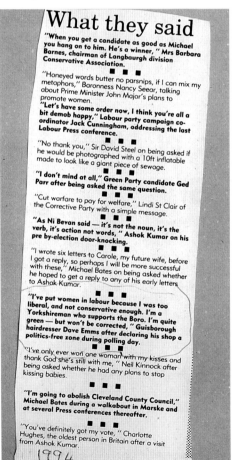

What they said

"When you get a candidate as good as Michael you hang on to him. He's a winner," Mrs Barbara Barnes, chairman of Langbaurgh division Conservative Association.

■ ■ ■

"Honeyed words butter no parsnips, if I can mix my metaphors," Baronness Nancy Seear, talking about Prime Minister John Major's plans to promote women.

"Let's have some order now, I think you're all a bit demob happy," Labour party campaign co-ordinator Jack Cunningham, addressing the last Labour Press conference.

■ ■ ■

"No thank you," Sir David Steel on being asked if he would be photographed with a 10ft inflatable made to look like a giant piece of sewage.

■ ■ ■

"I don't mind at all," Green Party candidate Ged Parr after being asked the same question.

■ ■ ■

"Cut warfare to pay for welfare," Lindi St Clair of the Corrective Party with a simple message.

■ ■ ■

"As Ni Bevan said — it's not the noun, it's the verb, it's action not words," Ashok Kumar on his pre by-election door-knocking.

■ ■ ■

"I wrote six letters to Carole, my future wife, before I got a reply, so perhaps I will be more successful with these," Michael Bates on being asked whether he hoped to get a reply to any of his early letters to Ashok Kumar.

■ ■ ■

"I've put women in labour because I was too liberal, and not conservative enough. I'm a Yorkshireman who supports the Boro. I'm quite green — but won't be corrected," Guisborough hairdresser Dave Emms after declaring his shop a politics-free zone during polling day.

■ ■ ■

"I've only ever won one woman with my kisses and thank God she's still with me," Neil Kinnock after being asked whether he had any plans to stop kissing babies.

■ ■ ■

"I'm going to abolish Cleveland County Council," Michael Bates during a walkabout in Marske and at several Press conferences thereafter.

■ ■ ■

"You've definitely got my vote," Charlotte Hughes, the oldest person in Britain after a visit from Ashok Kumar.

1994

On the left is the Singing Cowboy for whom we have no name. Dave Emms is feeding the horse upon which Jill Lane sits, vainly attempting to cover herself with hair

A group of runners gather at The Starting Gate pub in Redcar for the Langbaurgh Half Marathon, ready to raise money for a wheelchair for Malcolm (number 580). Dave Emms is middle row left, number 303

May 2 1992. Already known for raising money for multiple sclerosis sufferers, Dave Emms and Wendy Dale decided, in conjunction with Redcar and District Lions, on a Slave Auction for their next venture. Dressed in their Roman togas Dave and Wendy raffled their services for a day...

Slave sale, day of the 'draw', 2 July 1992. Seated on the left is Pauline Shorten, then Barry Shorten, with Wendy Dale and Dave Emms on the podium, awaiting their fate

On the day that the winning raffle ticket was drawn Dave and Wendy were won by Mrs Bow who ordered them to do a 'pub crawl' in Redcar, collecting more money for multiple sclerosis.

Dave says that was a very hard task, but I'm sure his tongue is in his cheek!

*

Shortly after this event Dave himself was diagnosed with multiple sclerosis.

In 1994 Dave, by now confined to a wheelchair, was overheard bemoaning the fact that he could no longer walk up the hills. The Cleveland Mountain Rescue Team, as a thank you for the money he had raised in the past, stepped in with an offer he couldn't resist:

How did he fancy being thrown off Highcliff?

Never one to miss an opportunity Dave says he jumped at the chance (metaphorically speaking!) and was taken to the top of the hills, strapped tightly into a rescue stretcher and lowered down the side of Highcliff. To the rescue team it was all part of a day's work, but to Dave it was a day that will never be forgotten.

June 8 1994. Dave Emms is strapped into a rescue stretcher and lowered down the side of Highcliff by the Cleveland Mountain Rescue team

Barber's charity cliff plunge

A GUISBOROUGH barber was "thrown" 70ft off a cliff as a thank-you for his charity work!

David Emms, who suffers from multiple sclerosis, can no longer walk on the hills on his own, so he jumped at the chance to be taken up High Cliff to take part in a Cleveland Search and Rescue Team exercise.

Dave has raised hundreds of pounds for the team and other charities and was sponsored for his effort last night.

Strapped

He was strapped in a Bell mountain rescue stretcher before being lowered down the rock face on two ropes.

Dave raised £200, half of which is going to the search and rescue team and half to a multiple sclerosis research charity.

The Guisborough Pageant of 18 July 1951 was a splendid and colourful affair with actors and dancers from the town recreating history.

The Priory formed the backdrop for scenes of the foundations of Whitby Abbey and Guisborough Priory, Elizabethan Court scenes, dances and madrigals, and tributes to Captain James Cook.

Scene 5 included John Wesley who visited Guisborough several times; William Wilberforce who fought for the abolition of the slave trade and who contributed funds towards the founding of Providence School; the marking of the fact that it was one hundred years since the beginning of the ironstone mining; and the silver jubilee of Queen Victoria.

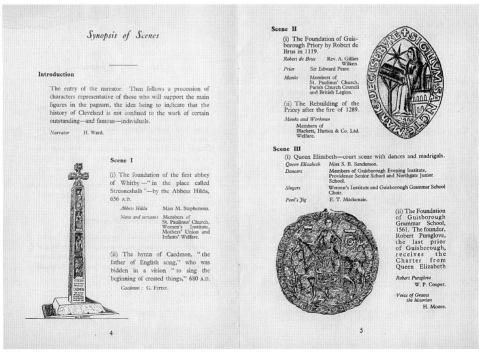

Although unconfirmed, this is likely to have been the young man who portrayed Caedmon, G Ferrer

Elizabethan courtiers preparing to dance, but the only one who can be identified is Norman Jeffels, second from left

Back row, second from left is Walter Jeffels, then Ida Jeffels, and second from right Mrs Kitchen from Pinchinthorpe. Front row left to right: Barbara Jeffels, then one of Dr Pratt's daughters

(right) Harrison Decorators on Redcar Road provides the backdrop for a group of slaves during the 1951 Pageant.

From left to right are Ann Hewling, Wilson Weatherhead and Brian Walker; wielding the whip is the slavemaster, Mr Page.

Ida Jeffels and Christine Hill in beautiful dresses, provided for the occasion by Sir Edward and Lady Pease

(right) Norman Jeffels at the back of the family shop in the late nineteen-thirties. The Jeffels family are remembered by many people in Guisborough for their various shops.

The business began in 1919 when Thomas John Jeffels moved to Guisborough from Cowton and started his first grocery shop next to the Mermaid Inn.

He had seven sons and three daughters and out of them all, three sons and a daughter eventually became shopkeepers themselves.

Norman Jeffels sitting on the bumper of the shop van

In 1937, as part of the Coronation Celebrations, a sporting event was held. Bill Nicholson (below) won first prize in the high jump.

Bill Nicholson during the Coronation Celebrations in 1937

A Smashing Time on Fountain Street

In the late nineteen-sixties a piano-smashing competition was held to raise money for the charity 'Guide Dogs for the Blind'. Standing by, camera in hand, was Edmund Phillips...

The audience assembles on Fountain Street car park while the organ grinder takes a rest

The crowds dig deep in aid of 'Guide Dogs for the Blind'

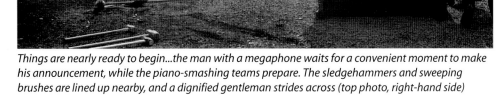

Things are nearly ready to begin...the man with a megaphone waits for a convenient moment to make his announcement, while the piano-smashing teams prepare. The sledgehammers and sweeping brushes are lined up nearby, and a dignified gentleman strides across (top photo, right-hand side)

(Other notable features in this photograph are the Sparrow Lane footbridge over the railway line—left-hand side, middle distance—and the view of Blackett Hutton, now demolished. By 2005 this area was home to an office block, a health centre, a DIY superstore and a Council office)

The writing on the hammer says 'Guisborough Round Table Guide Dogs for the Blind'. In the background we can see the vertical sign of the Carlton cinema—the building that started life as the Temperance Hall

Let the action begin...the crowds keep well back as the dust and splinters fly. (This photograph shows the Guisborough Gas Works at an interesting point in its history. A new high-pressure tank (far left) had just been installed, and soon afterwards the two large gas holders were removed. By 1967 demolition was complete. The two-storey brick building to the right of the high-pressure tank was the Gas Works office)

The big tidy-up! Alan Dawson (far left) and Alan Dale (far right) pose with two smashing friends of theirs

Chapter 3

Schools and Colleges

Guisborough Grammar School teachers in 1928. Left to right are H Lowes, Miss Emerson, L Savage, T F H Berwick, I Thomas and D Bragg

Guisborough Grammar School in 1928, Form II. Left to right (back row): Dack, Corner, A Smith, Harpley, Dadd, Riley, Walton, Barnard, K A Bell; (middle row): K Parkin, Chisholm II, Tyreman, Harrison, Wilkinson, Buxton, Blenkey, Snow; (front row): J Brunton, Allen, R Frankland

Providence Infant and Junior School in 1922. Somewhere on the back row is 'Sonny' Easby

Providence School in the late nineteen-twenties. Third from the left on the front row, next to the teacher, sits Mary Easby, later Mary Brown, who is remembered by a generation of Guisborough schoolchildren (now reaching their forties) as the school nurse. The girls had a very good team of Folk Dancers and were taken to compete in the Festival at Whitby each year by Miss Goodwill, the teacher. In 1928, the time of this photograph, the school log for July 13 records that 'Lady Gisborough has invited the schoolchildren this afternoon (after school) to the new playing field in Belmangate which she is giving them'

Providence School in the early nineteen-fifties. Those identified include Pamela Nixon, Marcia Brown, Mrs Cooper, Mona Collinson, Susan Mollan and John England (back row, far left)

Providence School Boys' yard in 1950. From left to right are Brian Boyes, John Wilkinson, Wilson Weatherhead, Derek Fisher, and front left to right are Terry Abrahams, Des Swales and Dennis Hastings

Country dancing in the school yard at Providence. Mill House can be seen very clearly in the background. From left to right are: Joan Hodgson, Joan McGuire, Mary Smith, Rosemary Nicholson, Joan Brown, Pauline Easton, Elaine Fawcett, Jennifer Hurn, Maureen Duff, Barbara Jackson, Jean Meadows, Greta Boyes, Pat Blake, Audrey Lightburn, Mary Hall, Beryl Kerr, Ann Milburn and Jean Mudd

Guisborough Senior School 1951 Form 3A. Back row left to right: Brian Thorpe, Jackie Dale, Gilbert Leather, Brian Wilson, Tony Briggs, Peter Dunn, Michael Calvert, Freddie Bowmaker, Kenneth Simpson, John Baynes, Bobby Beck, Brian Clark. Third row left to right: Gordon Parkin, Alan Young, Bessie Gill, Ann Milburn, Elaine Fawcett, Brenda Muir, Maureen Stamper, Maureen Peacock, Maureen Milward, Olive Swan, Rosemary Nicholson, Kenneth Allen, Kenneth Kidd. Second row left to right: Lily Clements, Beryl Kerr, Pauline Easton, Audrey Lightburn, Barbara Jackson, Pauline Hackleton, Mary Hall, Joyce Ward, Joan Pattison, Betty Walton, Jean Mudd. Front row left to right: Charlie Drury, Arthur Hurn, Billy Watson, Eric Richardson

Margrove Park School Sports Day, 1969, boys' race. Left to right: Andrew Drinkhall, -?-, Philip Eddon, Russell Teasdale, Michael Barnes

Margrove Park School Sports Day, 1969, girls' race. Left to right: Elaine Wynn, Pauline Barnes, -?-, Corrine Fairbanks, -?-, -?-

Margrove Park School Christmas Party, 1966. Headteacher Alma Robinson is on the far right

Margrove Park School, 1970. From left: Brian Barnes, Ian Watson, Neil Porritt, Glen Porritt, Santa Claus

Northgate Juniors 1950–1. Back from left; Brian Westacott, Peter Muir, Jimmy Davidson, Peter Milward, Edwin Petler, John Dale, Terry Bailey, David Flower, Roger Sutcliffe, Robert Sigsworth, George Pattison. Next row; Joe Booth, Doris Garbutt, Joan Hale, Barbara Watson, Barbara Baines, Barbara Marshall, Pat Curtain, Margaret Lampley, Pamela Dowson, Joan Wilson, Margaret Dale, Margaret Lewis, Barry Claxton. Next row; Vera Parkin, Maureen Dunkley, Irene Clements, Ann Storey, Elaine Redman, Margaret Clements, Barbara Nicholson, Dorothy Smith, Kathleen Pearson. Front row; Tony Bennett, Francis Dadd, John Brookes, Robert Pattison, Keith Abraham, Jimmy Calvert, Barry Cleaver, John Swainston, Brian Carter

Laurence Jackson School teachers in the late nineteen-seventies including Mr Fairbanks, Mr Marshall, Mr Martin, Mr Barnard, Mrs Clamp, Mr Ward, Mr Tomlinson, Mr Bramham, Mr Duggan, Mrs Newson, Mr Matuszak, Mr Downs, Mr Woodall, Mr Johnson, Mr Appleby, Mr Cloughton, Mr Brodrick, Mr Hewitt, Mr Webb, Mr Hartley, Mr Madgin, Mr Young, Mr Turner, Mrs Matuszak, Mrs Curry, Miss Guest, Mrs Potts, Mrs Cross, Mrs Newton, Miss Campbell, Mrs Brighton, Miss Ditchfield, Mrs Powley, Mrs Chambers, Mrs Redshaw, Mrs Clamp, Mr Cox, Mrs Stanley, Mr Cottler, Mr Harrison, Mr Morgan, Mr Henderson, Mr Halpin, Mr Mackenzie, Mrs Cowton, Mr Brelstaff

Chapter 4

The Lost Mansion

The south front of Park House facing Highcliff and Roseberry Topping (W D Brelstaff, 1968)

The north side of Park House showing the adjacent buildings. The smaller seventeenth-century house on the right, believed to be contemporary with Park House, is currently used as a barn (W D Brelstaff)

Park House—a brief history

By 1540 Guisborough Priory had been surrendered to Henry VIII in the Dissolution and its wealth transferred to the Crown—ending more than 400 years of religious tradition. The buildings were soon to be demolished and used as building stone.

The first lessee of the site, Thomas Leigh, was not given permission to carry away any stone, nor was the second lessee, Thomas Chaloner. However, Chaloner purchased the site in 1550, and this time he bought the rights to reuse or sell the buildings for scrap.

It is not known how much of the Priory had been dismantled by Henry VIII in the ten years between 1540 and 1550, but evidently there was plenty left. Even in the early seventeenth century, stone from the Priory was being used in Chaloner's alum works.

By 1600 the Chaloner family, originally from London, began to take an active interest in the Guisborough area, and formed the Alum Company in 1606. But it was not until 1655 that Sir Edward, ancestor of the present Chaloners in Guisborough, moved to the area.

Sir Edward Chaloner is believed to have built Park House in 1660, soon after his arrival. It is not known whether any Priory stone was used in the construction of Park House.

The north front of Park House facing the coast and sea, and Eston hills to the west (behind the photographer). Note the unusual chimney stacks, one with a fourth flue tacked on (W D Brelstaff, 1968)

Sir Edward was succeeded by his son William Chaloner (1655–1715) in 1680. William did not stay long at Park House; he built a new manor house in Bow Street, known as the 'Old Hall'. This became the Chaloner family's residence until 1817 when it was sold off as a result of bankruptcy. The family then moved to Long Hull, a farm on Whitby Lane, which was later rebuilt and extended. In 1902 that building was renamed Gisborough Hall.

From 1700 onwards Park House was held mostly by tenants until its demolition in 1970.

The exterior of the house was much altered—the windows were a mix of original stone mullions (blocked up), early Georgian sashes, Victorian sashes and twentieth-century casements. The interior was drastically partitioned; the Chaloners retained the dining room for use by shooting parties (W D Brelstaff)

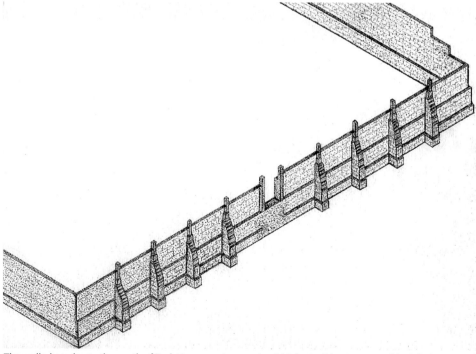

The walled garden to the south of Park House: an impressive 144-feet-wide structure with eight buttressed pillars and carved stonework. The garden had lawns on two levels and doorways to the park (Paul Smith)

By 1968 Park House was untenanted, derelict and abandoned (W D Brelstaff)

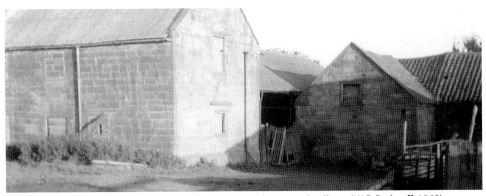

Windows on these outbuildings indicate former use as domestic dwellings (W D Brelstaff, 1968)

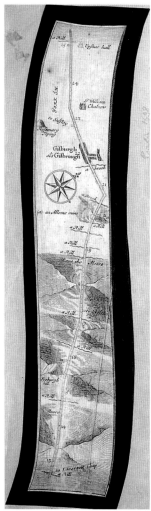

The south front of Park House (W D Brelstaff, 1968)

(above) By 1968 Park House was uninhabited.

(left) A 1698 strip map by John Ogilby, from the collection of the late W D Brelstaff. At the top of the map is shown Upsall Hall, with Park House below it on the right (a tiny sketch of Park House, annotated 'Sir William Chaloner'). Other notable references on the map include 'Rosemary Toping', 'Stoksley', 'Gisburgh or Gisbrough', 'an Allome mine', 'the Moore', 'Skelton Castle', 'Freburgh Hill',

A 1698 strip map by John Ogilby   and several references to 'a Hill' and 'a brook'.

A seventeenth-century dwelling near Park House (Paul Smith)

The projecting bays on the north and south are said to have had towers originally (W D Brelstaff)

The north front ground-floor window. Broken stonework flanking the head of the window (and a staircase inside) suggest that this was originally an entrance and porchway (W D Brelstaff, 1968)

Park House, 1660–1970

Among the roots and leaves of beech
Beneath the branches out of reach
Like driftwood scattered on a beach
Lie ruins on the floor

Beyond and further through the trees
Past bluebells hidden from the breeze
Are capstones piled in twos and threes
Like casualties of war

The gradient increases more
Ascending with the forest floor
Like those who came this way before
Returning from the park

Three hundred years this building stood
A manor house of stone and wood
A monument to sweat and blood
Now crumbling in the dark

A buttressed wall is all that stands
In memory of masons' hands
Who first surveyed these hunting lands
When Charles the Second reigned

Each sandstone buttress three feet wide
Displays a pattern etched with pride
Where art and function coincide
And balance is maintained

Eight buttresses provide support
Spread out along the stony fort
Like guardians of an ancient court
Now vanquished and betrayed

And in the centre on the floor
Wrought iron gates and stone galore
The stairway to an ancient door
Now broken and decayed

Beyond the wall a garden grew
With terraced lawns and feverfew
For Chaloners a dazzling view
Not many could command

The southern aspect of the hills
Would compensate for many ills
While alum mining paid the bills
And tenants worked the land

In 1660 give or take
A year or two for history's sake
The artisans began to make
A home fit for a lord

Park House was built before St Paul's
Such things discussed within its walls
Bubonic plague and Tudor halls
The warring Dutch abroad

The Fire of London came and went
And then the Dutch invaded Kent
As Park House capital was spent
On furniture and frills

Two towers on the back and front
Would house observers of the hunt
While in the grounds the roe deer grunt
And scamper to the hills

The house was large and strongly made
With massive flues and colonnade
The buttressed wall a barricade
Against the Yorkshire grime

With fourteen fires maybe more
Three storeys high reduced from four
A sundial built above the door
To measure out the time

For centuries the walls stood fast
The masons' work was made to last
But sadly this is in the past
For now the house is gone

Neglect compounded wear and tear
Abandonment and disrepair
Such disrespect and lack of care
Were shown by everyone

The early nineteen-seventies
Brought demolition through the trees
And smashed the building to its knees
Then threw it down the hill

Yet close in by the buttressed wall
You sometimes hear a hunter's call
And ghostly voices from the hall
Who can't forgive the wreckers' ball
And may go hunting still...

by Paul Smith

Last Train to Guisborough

On Saturday 29 February 1964 the last passenger train arrived in Guisborough. On board was Maurice Burns, a fresh-faced 17-year-old from Fairfield, Stockton-on-Tees, who borrowed his father's camera, spent his pocket money on a roll of 35mm film then cycled to Guisborough to record the final hours of the branch.

The film was developed in his darkroom which he made from a coalhouse, and the photographs remained in store and unseen for 40 years—until March 2004.

Maurice's photographs were exhibited in Guisborough Library to mark the 40th anniversary of the closure; this is the first time his collection has been published.

About Maurice Burns the Photographer

The recording of the sad images of this railway closure to Guisborough and many others in the North East left a lasting impression on the photographer.

The railways were here one day and then the tracks were ripped up and the buildings demolished the next. Maurice subsequently became heavily involved in the railway preservation movement, joining the infant North Yorkshire Moors Railway Preservation Society then holding many positions including Director of a charity that saved several LNER steam locomotives. As their Chief Mechanical Engineer he led teams of volunteers from all walks of life and returned steam engines to full working order. These included the famous *Blue Peter* and other LNER classes J27, Q6, Q7, J72 and K1. Some of these classes may have operated on the Guisborough branch from time to time. Maurice was fireman on the NYMR's very first public passenger train and served the Railway Trust for 25 years as a fireman and steam driver.

The story of Guisborough railway is a fascinating one, and a mystery to many people who arrived here after the branch had closed. To create a fuller picture of the railway we include in this chapter many other photographs, some of which show the town as it was before the housing estates were built. These photographs are from private collections, and are compiled with help from Maurice Burns, Geoff Scurr, Nick Carter, Mark Lloyd and I Harrington.

A Brief History

Guisborough railway opened in 1853 for mineral traffic (ironstone) and in 1854 for passenger traffic. It provided service for 110 years until the Beeching Report of the nineteen-sixties confirmed that it was losing money: the running costs were £15,300 per year; revenue was £6,700 per year. This justified closure on the grounds that it was unprofitable. But in retrospect, with the subsequent major expansion of Guisborough, was the closure a mistake...?

The small print states that: 'The Minister of Transport having sanctioned the withdrawal of the passenger Train Services from the above line, these services will be discontinued on and from 2nd March, 1964, and the following stations closed for passenger traffic: HUTTON GATE, GUISBOROUGH. Freight traffic will continue to be dealt with at Guisborough Station'. As there was no Sunday service, this meant that the effective last day of operation was Saturday 29 February 1964 (Maurice Burns)

A crowded 9.55am train from Guisborough at Middlesbrough Station on the last day (Maurice Burns)

Another view of the Guisborough train, the 12.15pm, departing Middlesbrough Station on the last day of services (Maurice Burns)

The train to Guisborough departed from Middlesbrough Station and passed through Ormesby, Nunthorpe and Hutton Gate before arriving at Guisborough Station—just 20 minutes later if it was on schedule. This chapter recreates the train's journey, using both 'last day' photographs and archive pictures to illustrate the complete route...

Middlesbrough shoppers on the last passenger train to Guisborough (Maurice Burns)

Climbing up to Ormesby Station on the last day of services to Guisborough (Maurice Burns)

Ormesby Station on the last day. Note the hopper wagons for the delivery of coal (Maurice Burns)

Ormesby Station before the buildings were demolished, looking up the bank towards Nunthorpe (photograph by R Coulthard)

Ormesby Station in the nineteen-sixties. The building was later demolished and replaced by a car park (see below), and the station renamed Marton (Ken Taylor)

Ormesby Station in 2005—the building has gone and the Station is renamed 'Marton' (Paul Smith)

Ormesby coal yard. Notice the neatly stacked coal sacks and the empty coal merchant's Ford Thames Trader wagon on the weighbridge (Maurice Burns)

Ormesby signal box, long since demolished— looking back down the bank towards Ormesby Station (Maurice Burns)

The gradient board at Nunthorpe coal yard indicates the steep (in railway terms) 1 in 44 incline into Nunthorpe Station. Behind is a wagon used for coal deliveries (Maurice Burns)

Nunthorpe Station—the top of Ormesby Bank is now behind the train in the distance. The section on the left is now the location of the car park, and the train is going over the level crossing (Maurice Burns)

Nunthorpe Station in 2005. The building still exists but the outside waiting area and adjoining structure have been demolished and replaced with a brick shelter (Paul Smith)

Nunthorpe Station on the last day of services to Guisborough (Maurice Burns)

After leaving Nunthorpe Station the train soon arrives at Nunthorpe East Junction. From here the Battersby line branches off to the right and the Guisborough line continues straight on. The car behind the fence is a Standard Vanguard (Maurice Burns)

Nunthorpe East Junction in 2005. The Battersby line is still used by the Middlesbrough to Whitby train but the Guisborough line was removed after closure in 1964. The concrete coal bunker, fence posts and crossing are still in place. The signal box is no longer there but its foundations remain (Paul Smith)

Looking back towards Nunthorpe East Junction. The Battersby line going to the left is still in use by the Esk Valley Railway on its 36-mile Middlesbrough to Whitby service. This travels over the moors via Marton (formerly 'Ormesby'), Gypsy Lane, Nunthorpe, Great Ayton, Battersby, Kildale, Commondale, Castleton Moor, Danby, Lealholm, Glaisdale, Egton, Grosmont, Sleights and Ruswarp (Maurice Burns)

Approximately two miles from Nunthorpe East Junction, just before Pinchinthorpe Station, the remains of a signal box marks the site of the former Chaloner junction. Here, a mineral line crossed the fields to the north and came out near the old Guisborough to Middlesbrough road, on its way to the ironstone mines. In the far distance is the road bridge at Pinchinthorpe Station (Geoff Scurr collection)

This view, showing the shortened and reroofed signal box, is looking back in the direction of Nunthorpe East Junction. The building still exists and is used for storage (Geoff Scurr collection)

Chaloner line crossing-keeper's hut on the old Middlesbrough–Guisborough road (Geoff Scurr collection)

Windle Bridge on the Middlesbrough to Guisborough main road was built to allow road traffic to cross over the Cleveland Railway (Geoff Scurr collection)

Back on the Guisborough line, a train bound for Scarborough enters Pinchinthorpe Station. Note the topiary in the shape of houses and the railway cottages just visible behind (Geoff Scurr collection)

A postcard view of Pinchingthorpe Station (renamed Pinchinthorpe on 1 April 1920) dating from 1905. This was the 'new' station that opened in 1876 to replace the older one on the other side of the bridge. The new station was closed to both freight and passengers on 24 October 1951. The road bridge was a 1916 replacement for an extremely busy level crossing: as many as 55 trains set off each day from mines around Guisborough, many using this line, as well as passenger trains and 55 trains of 'empties'!

The 'new' Pinchinthorpe Station seen in 1964 after closure. The original station that operated from 1854 to 1876 is just beyond the bridge carrying the road from Guisborough to Great Ayton (Maurice Burns)

Pinchinthorpe waiting room, still existing today, has now found a new use as a depot for the Countryside Wardens (Maurice Burns)

The gradient profile and 1/4 mile post on the approach to the road bridge, and a Volkswagen Beetle in the car park on the left-hand side of the track. The 'old' station is visible on the right (Maurice Burns)

The original Pinchinthorpe Station, built in 1854 and replaced in 1876. The present-day Walkway Centre and car park are a short distance from here on the left-hand side (Maurice Burns)

Approaching Hutton Gate Station from Pinchinthorpe, along the route of the present-day 'walkway'. The sign ahead, reflected in the carriage window, reads 'WHISTLE' (Maurice Burns)

Hutton Gate Station in 1955. The short siding visible on the right of the track was previously used for timber extraction. The signal box can be seen at the far end of the platform on the left (Photo Stations UK)

Hutton Gate waiting room in the mid-nineteen-sixties, around the time of closure (Mark Lloyd)

Hutton Gate after closure. The wooden crossing is now the road to Pease Court (Mark Lloyd)

Another view of Hutton Gate Station, this one apparently showing the Station house boarded up. The house still exists, unaltered, but the platform is now replaced by a garden (Mark Lloyd)

Stone-ballasted track at Hutton Gate Station looking towards Guisborough shortly after closure. The new ballast marks the site of a crossover track removed following closure of the signal box (Maurice Burns)

Hutton Gate Station on the last day of passenger services to Guisborough. Note that the signal box is missing: this was demolished some time before the line closed (Maurice Burns)

Departing Hutton Gate for Guisborough on the last day. These platforms still exist in the undergrowth, though a fence across the track marks the boundary of the former stationhouse garden (Maurice Burns)

This photograph is taken looking down the platform towards Guisborough. The gated track now leads to Pease Court, and the houses visible on the left are Hutton Lane and The Grove. The Avenue is directly to the left, out of shot (Maurice Burns)

A view of the mineral branch line that ran to Belmont ironstone mine at the top of Hunters Hill. The track in the foreground branched off the main Guisborough line at the point where Aldenham Road now crosses the track. The mineral line was abandoned in the early twentieth century and by the nineteen-sixties nature was reclaiming the embankment. Visible in the middle-distance is the concrete bridge (still existing, minus its arch). In the far distance are the brick buildings of Belmont mine (Ken Taylor)

A few hundred yards further along are the signals on the approach to Guisborough signal box. The houses on the left are on the Hutton Lane estate, which was built in 1963. The stone gate post on the far side of the track still exists. In the distance, roughly in line with the present-day allotment site, can be seen the large signal post—this stood in front of the area now cut through by Enfield Chase. This area is easily recognisable today, although the Hunters Hill estate is now visible to the right (Mark Lloyd)

Further along, just before the area where Enfield Chase now crosses the route of the railway line, is Guisborough Junction—with the branch line on the left heading off towards the station. The allotments on the left-hand side still exist, and Hunters Hill estate is now on the right-hand side (Maurice Burns)

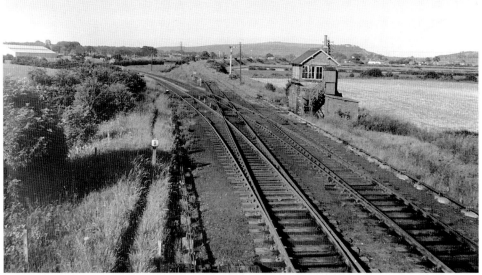

Nearer to the signal box the branch line is clearly visible on the left. This area is now cut through by Enfield Chase; Hunters Hill was built on the fields to the right. In the distance the line continues on to Brotton and Loftus—this section had been closed to passenger traffic from 3 May 1960, the day the Middlesbrough to Loftus service was cut back to Guisborough (Maurice Burns)

Close-up of the signals at Guisborough Junction that controlled all lines into Guisborough (Mark Lloyd)

Class A8 steam engine—the mainstay motive power for the Guisborough branch (Geoff Scurr collection)

This close-up view shows the signal box in more detail. In the distance, just visible between the drainpipe and the signal post, is the mineral line embankment that served the Belmont ironstone mine

Guisborough signal box—originally called Hutton Junction until it was renamed on 16 March 1932. The farmland in the background is now the Hunters Hill estate (Maurice Burns)

The signalman at Guisborough Junction working the last shift for passenger services on 29 February 1964. Note the tidiness of the cabin right to the very last shift—the highly polished stove, coal fire and boiling kettle for tea! (Maurice Burns)

A view of the branch line diagram above the levers that control the signals and points inside the Guisborough signal box (Maurice Burns)

The highly polished levers inside Guisborough signal box on the last shift (Maurice Burns)

Approaching Sparrow Lane bridge on the way into Guisborough Station. In the nineteen-sixties this area still showed evidence of the older Cleveland Railway that had long since merged with the Stockton & Darlington line. The stone construction (left) was part of a disused bridge (John Linton collection)

The Sparrow Lane bridge over the branch line just outside the station (Mark Lloyd)

Pedestrians walking along Sparrow Lane from Rectory Lane would first walk across the bridge on the opposite page (to cross the branch line) then walk under the above bridge that once carried the line to Boosbeck and beyond. In the distance are the open fields of Hunters Hill Farm (now a housing estate) and beyond them the site of the former Belmont ironstone mine (Mark Lloyd)

This nineteen-fifties photograph shows a steam train to Whitby hauled by a Gresley Class A8 locomotive. Also in the picture is part of a bridge or similar structure, possibly relics left over from the Cleveland Railway (J W Armstrong)

This photograph was taken from the top of the Sparrow Lane overbridge. The Priory arch is visible in the distance and on the left are the sidings leading to Blackett Hutton foundry (Maurice Burns)

The entry to Guisborough Station. At the extreme right of the picture can be seen the chimneys of the Chaloner Hospital; on the extreme left are the houses along Fountain Street. In the distance, behind the Station, are the trees along Bow Street (Maurice Burns)

In this late nineteen-fifties scene, Thornaby shed's L1 class tank engine 67754 propels its train back to Guisborough Junction before heading to Loftus and Whitby via the coast route (John Linton collection)

Looking from Guisborough Station towards the Sparrow Lane bridge and the Guisborough Junction signal box beyond. Photograph taken on 29 February 1964, the last day of services (I Harrington)

The goods facilities at Guisborough—a hand-operated crane. The last afternoon train is departing in the distance and has just passed the Weigh Cabin (Maurice Burns)

A close-up view of the crane showing the winding handle at the rear (Mark Lloyd)

Guisborough Goods Shed viewed from the rear. The sign on the right-hand shed reads 'BIBBY Cakes, Meals and Ley-Test Poultry Foods' (Mark Lloyd)

Inside the Goods Shed a goods van is used for storing sacks. A sign on the door reads 'NOT TO LEAVE GUISBOROUGH', and the number is 040008 (Mark Lloyd)

The loco shed, seen here on the right-hand side of the picture, was closed in 1953 (J W Armstrong)

The Weigh Cabin at Guisborough Station, used for weighing coal. The sign above the window reads 'NOTICE, ALL COAL TO BE PAID FOR ON DELIVERY'. The metal weighing platform is set into the road adjacent to the building on the left-hand side of the picture, beneath the large window (Mark Lloyd)

Guisborough Station after closure, at the start of demolition (note the ladder) (Mark Lloyd)

A solitary goods van awaits removal after the station is closed (Mark Lloyd)

Guisborough Station in the nineteen-thirties showing the bay platform on the right which allowed two trains to be in the station at the same time. The double-bracket lower quadrant signals would control the departures (Ken Taylor)

Guisborough Station in 1955—the topiary and decorative plants were a common sight at railway stations in the nineteen-fifties (Photo Stations UK)

In the early nineteen-sixties the non-availability of the usual diesel multiple units saw the branch return to steam haulage for one day. In this view, Thornaby shed's LNER class V3 no. 67640 reverses out of the station prior to running round its coaches and returning to Middlesbrough. Note the old four-wheeled barrow on the left used for carrying luggage or parcels (Ken Linford)

A father and daughter, having watched locomotive 67640 'change ends', return to the station (Ken Linford)

Guisborough Station in 1957. Note the broken glass in the roof caused no doubt by the heat from the steam locomotives! This is seen on all photographs from 1955 to 1964. Note also the glass draught screen behind the seat—this was later removed (compare it to the photograph below, taken in the nineteen-sixties). Photograph by Hugh Davies ('Photos from the Fifties')

Guisborough Station on the last day. The name board on the seat is marked 'GUISBOROUGH'; the board on the floor to the left of the train warns: 'no ENGINE or VAN to pass this BOARD' (Maurice Burns)

The Guisborough Station nameboard (Maurice Burns)

A view of a steam train entering Guisborough Station in the nineteen-fifties. Photograph by David Lawrence ('Photos from the Fifties')

Arriving at Guisborough on the morning train from Middlesbrough, on the last day. On the right can be seen the base of the former steam-engine shed (Maurice Burns)

The front of the station showing the Goods Shed entrance on the left and the dead end through the station (Maurice Burns)

Guisborough Station on the last day, seen from the Bow Street entrance. The notice board on the door reads 'Notice to Passengers. Tickets are not issued at this station but can be obtained from the guard of the train. Passengers are requested to travel in the rear two coaches and those travelling beyond Middlesbrough kindly inform the guard on joining the train' (Maurice Burns)

The Bow Street entrance to Guisborough Station on the last day of passenger services. The closure notice seen at the beginning of this chapter is at the base of the signpost, just out of sight behind the picket fencing on the right. This area is now the entrance to the Health Centre (Maurice Burns)

The stationhouse and yard from the Bow Street entrance, looking towards Chaloner Street (Mark Lloyd)

A 1955 photograph of the Stationmaster's house and the adjoining public entrance (Photo Stations UK)

Guisborough Station and Stationmaster's house, with a Ford Anglia parked outside (Mark Lloyd)

The station's public entrance and canopy. Notice that the glazed roof windows are the same design as those on the main train shed (Mark Lloyd)

A wide-angle view showing the unusual roof line of the station buildings (Mark Lloyd)

This 1955 view shows the inside of Guisborough Station, with the destination sign and clock clearly visible. The sign displays 'TRAIN for WHITBY'. In the distance are the buffer stops and beyond is Bow Street (Photo Stations UK)

Looking out of the station in the other direction, this photograph complements the one above—the pram, trolley and destination board would suggest they were contemporary (I Harrington collection)

The inside of the station—the sign for 'GENTLEMEN' is just visible! (Mark Lloyd)

A small figure stands in solitude, silhouetted in the entrance to Guisborough Station on the last day of passenger services (Maurice Burns)

The NER departure board at Guisborough Station on the last day (Maurice Burns)

Bargain day-return tickets—in shillings and pence! (Maurice Burns)

The hand-written departures notice on display in Guisborough Station (Maurice Burns)

At dusk the signals are pulled off for the last train, the 5.37pm, from Middlesbrough (note the lower quadrant in the distance). Soon the polished lines to the station would be no more (Maurice Burns)

Last-day mourner John Hardy, assisting the Guisborough signalman by placing the lit oil lamp behind the signal lens. John later became volunteer stationmaster at Grosmont on the North York Moors Railway (Maurice Burns)

The Middlesbrough train departing Guisborough on the last day of services (Maurice Burns)

The train for Middlesbrough departs Guisborough on the last day of services (Maurice Burns)

Table 34

Table 34

SCARBOROUGH, WHITBY, GUISBOROUGH and MIDDLESBROUGH

WEEKDAYS ONLY

Miles	Miles	Station		am	am	am	am	am	am	SX pm	SO pm	am	pm	pm	SX pm	pm	pm	pm	SO pm
		32 York	dep	..	..	..	..	..	..	..	..	am 10 15	..	pm 1 36	..	..	pm 3 18	pm 6 16	..
—		SCARBOROUGH (Cen.)	dep	..	..	..	..	..	..	..	..	11 45	..	2 47	..	..	4 26	7 55	..
5		Cloughton	"	..	..	..	..	..	..	..	..	12 5	..	3 4	..	..	4 41	8 10	..
7		Hayburn Wyke ‡	"	..	..	..	..	..	..	..	..	12 9	..	3 8	..	..	4 45	8D14	..
8		Stainton Dale	"	..	..	..	..	..	..	..	..	12 12	..	3 11	..	..	4 48	8 17	..
10¼		Ravenscar	"	..	..	..	..	..	..	..	..	12 19	..	3 18	..	..	4 55	8 24	..
13½		Fyling Hall ‡	"	..	..	..	..	..	..	..	..	12 26	..	3 25	..	..	5 2	8D31	..
15¼		Robin Hood's Bay	"	..	..	..	..	..	..	..	..	12 30	..	3 29	..	..	5 6	8 35	..
18½		Hawsker	"	..	..	..	..	..	..	..	..	12 38	..	3 37	..	..	5b14	8 43	..
23½		Whitby (Town)	arr	..	..	..	..	..	..	..	..	12 51	..	3 50	..	..	5 27	8 56	..
			dep	..	6 55	..	..	..	10 30	..	..	12 55	..	4 8	..	..	5 35	..	9 15
25		Ruswarp	"	..	6 58	..	..	..	10 33	..	..	12 58	..	4 11	..	..	5 38	..	9 18
26½		Sleights	"	..	7 2	..	..	..	10 37	..	..	1 2	..	4 15	..	..	5 42	..	9 22
		32 York	dep	..	4 30	..	..	..	..	..	..	10 28	..	1 36	..	..	3 18	..	..
29¾		Grosmont	dep	..	7 10		..	..	10 45	..	..	1 10	..	4 23	..		5 50	..	9 30
31¼		Egton	"	..	7‡14		..	..	10 49	..	..	1 14	..	4 27	..		5‡54	..	9‡34
33		Glaisdale	"	..	7 19		..	..	10 55	..	..	1 20	..	4 31	..		5 58	..	9 38
35		Lealholm	"	..	7 24		..	..	11 0	..	..	1 25	..	4 36	..		6 3	..	..
38½		Danby	"	..	7 32	Through Train to Newcastle	..	..	11 7	..	..	1 32	..	4 43	..	Through Train and MB to Newcastle	6 10	..	..
40		Castleton	"	..	7 38		..	..	11 10	..	..	1 38	..	4 46	..		6 13	..	..
41¾		Commondale ‡	"	..	7 42		..	..	11 14	..	..	1 42	..	4 50	..		6 17	..	..
45¾		Kildale ‡	"	..	7 49		..	..	11 21	..	..	1 49	..	4 57	..		6 24	..	..
47½		Battersby	arr	..	7 53		..	..	11 25	..	..	1 53	..	5 1	..		6 28	..	..
			dep	..	7 58		..	..	11 29	..	..	1 57	..	5 5	..		6 32	..	..
50		Great Ayton ‡	"	..	8 4	..	..	..	11 35	..	..	2 3	..	5 11	..	..	6 38	..	..
—	—	Guisborough	"	7 30	..	8 12	8 30	9 55	..	1 30	1 45	..	4 28	..	5 42	6 10	..	..	..
—	1½	Hutton Gate ‡	"	7 34	..	8 16	8 34	9 59	..	1 34	1 49	..	4 32	..	5 46	6 14	..	..	..
54	5½	Nunthorpe	"	7 40	8 12	8 22	8 40	10 5	11 43	1 40	1 55	2 11	4 38	5 19	5 52	6 20	6 46	..	..
55½	7	Ormesby	"	7 44	8 16	8 26	8 44	10 9	11 47	1 44	1 59	2 15	4 42	5 23	5 56	6 24	6 50	..	..
58½	10	MIDDLESBROUGH	arr	7 50	8 22	8 32	8 50	10 15	11 53	1 50	2 5	2 21	4 48	5 30	6 2	6 31	6 56	..	..
—		38 Darlington	arr	8 28	8 56	9 12	9 26	10 56	12 26	2 29	..	2 58	5 28	6 28	6 56	..	7 26	..	..
—		42 Newcastle	"	..	..	10 1	10 59	11 59	1 59	..	..	3 59	..	7 0	..	8 0	9 0	..	..

For other trains between Whitby (Town) and Grosmont, see Table 32.

D—Calls to set down only
MB—Miniature Buffet Car.

SO—Saturdays only.
SX—Saturdays excepted.

b—No staff in attendance on Saturdays.
‡—No staff in attendance.

TO ORGANISERS OF PARTIES

British Railways offer the services of their own staff to help organisers of parties in arranging outings. On your behalf these experienced men, who specialise in this work, will arrange road sightseeing tours, admission to places of interest, meals in restaurants or packed meals for the journey, steamer trips, and any of the other attractions you may have in mind for your outing. In some towns they can arrange theatre bookings for you as well.

Call in the expert help of British Railways. It will cost you nothing, and it can make all the difference to the success of your outing. There is a Party Outings booklet giving details of popular itineraries. It will be sent free on request.

169

Trains departed Guisborough Station at 7.30am and arrived in Middlesbrough Station at 7.50am...

Table 34

Table 34—continued.

MIDDLESBROUGH, GUISBOROUGH, WHITBY and SCARBOROUGH

WEEKDAYS ONLY

Miles	Miles	Station	am	am	am	am	am	SO am/pm	SX am/pm	am/pm	pm	pm	SX pm	pm	pm
—	—	42 Newcastle .... dep	....	....	5 52	7 0	8 13	10 13	11 13	11 13	2 13	....	3 13	4 13	..
		38 Darlington .. .. ,,	6 15	6 45	..	8 15	9 15	11 45	11 45	12p15	3 15	3 45	4 15	4 45	5 15
		MIDDLESBROUGH .... dep	6 45	7 20	7 35	9 5	9 55	12 15	12 38	12 50	3 45	4 33	5 8	5 37	6 0
3	3	Ormesby .. .. ,,	6 51	7 27	7 41	9 11	10 1	12 21	12 44	12 56	3 51	4 39	5 14	5 43	6 6
4½	4½	Nunthorpe .. .. ,,	6 57	7 34	7 47	9 17	10 7	12 27	12 50	1 2	3 57	4 45	5 20	5 49	6 12
—	8½	Hutton Gate‡ .. ,,	7 4	..	7 54	9 24	..	12 34	12 57	..	4 4	..	5 27	5 56	..
—	10	Guisborough .... arr	7 8	..	7 58	9 28	..	12 38	1 1	..	4 8	..	5 31	6 0	..
8½		Great Ayton‡ .. dep	..	7 44	..	..	10 16	..	..	1 11	..	4 54	..	..	6 21
11		Battersby .... { arr	..	7 51	..	..	10 21	..	..	1 16	..	4 59	..	..	6 26
		{ dep	..	7 55	..	..	10 25	..	..	1 20	..	5 3	..	..	6 30
12½		Kildale ‡ .... ,,	..	8 0	..	..	10 30	..	..	1 25	..	5 8	..	..	6 35
16½		Commondale ‡ .. ,,	..	8 7	..	..	10 37	..	..	1 32	..	5 15	..	..	6 42
18½		Castleton .... ,,	..	8 12	..	..	10 41	..	..	1 36	..	5 19	..	..	6 46
20		Danby .. .. ,,	..	8 17	..	..	10 44	..	..	1 39	..	5 22	..	..	6 49
23½		Lealholm .. .. ,,	..	8 24	..	..	10 50	..	..	1 45	..	5 28	..	..	6 55
25½		Glaisdale .. .. ,,	..	8 29	..	..	10 54	..	..	1 49	..	5 32	..	..	6 59
27½		Egton .. .. ,,	..	8 33	..	..	10 58	..	..	1 53	..	5‡36	..	..	7‡ 4
28½		Grosmont .. .. ,,	..	8 37	..	..	11 2	..	..	1 57	..	5 40	..	..	7 8
—		32 York .... arr	....	11 1	....	..	1 22	....	....	....	....	....	....	..	8 57
32		Sleights .. .. dep	..	8 45	..	..	11 10	..	..	2 5	..	5 48	..	..	7 16
33½		Ruswarp .. .. ,,	..	8 49	..	..	11 14	..	..	2 9	..	5 52	..	..	7 20
35		Whitby (Town) ...... { arr	..	8 52	..	..	11 17	..	..	2 12	..	5 55	..	..	7 23
		{ dep	..	8 57	..	..	11 22	..	..	2 18	..	6 0	..	..	..
40		Hawsker .. ,,	..	9 11	..	..	11 36	..	..	2b32	..	6 14	..	..	..
43½		Robin Hood's Bay .... ,,	..	9 17	..	..	11 42	..	..	2 38	..	6 20	..	..	..
45		Fyling Hall ‡.. ,,	..	9 21	..	..	..	..	..	2 42	..	6D24	..	..	..
48½		Ravenscar .... ,,	..	9 30	..	..	11 53	..	..	2 51	..	6 33	..	..	..
50½		Stainton Dale .. ,,	..	9 35	..	..	11 58	..	..	2 56	..	6 38	..	..	..
51½		Hayburn Wyke ‡ .... ,,	..	9 38	..	..	..	..	..	2 59	..	6 41	..	..	..
53½		Cloughton .. ,,	..	9 41	..	..	12 3	..	..	3 6	..	6 44	..	..	..
58½		SCARBOROUGH (Cen.) arr	..	9 55	..	..	12 17	..	..	3 20	..	7 1	..	..	..
32		32 York .. .. arr	..	11 1	..	..	1 22	..	..	4 56	..	8 57	..	..	..

For other trains between Grosmont and Whitby (Town), see Table 32.

D—Calls to set down only.
MB—Miniature Buffet Car.

SO—Saturdays only.
SX—Saturdays excepted.

b—No staff in attendance on Saturdays.
p—pm.
‡—No staff in attendance.

DAY RETURN TICKETS

are issued between most stations within a wide radius and offer real reductions in fares.

Full details from stations and agencies.

170

...a mere twenty minutes later. And it only cost 2 shillings and 4 pence! If only this service existed today

An atmospheric view of some ghost-like figures inside Guisborough Station (Maurice Burns)

The driver's view of the train departing Guisborough (Maurice Burns)

As dusk falls at 6pm on 29 February 1964 we see the very last train to Guisborough passing the junction signal box (Maurice Burns)

In the fading light the last train stands at Guisborough prior to departure at 6.10pm (Maurice Burns)

Beyond Guisborough Junction the line continues on to Spawood, Slapewath, Boosbeck and onwards to Loftus and Whitby. Services along this section had ceased in 1960 but the line was still passable until the tracks were lifted some years later. The next few pages contain archive photographs of the journey between Guisborough and Slapewath...

This photograph was taken in August 1964 from the Sparrow Lane area looking towards Guisborough Junction signal box. The Hutton Lane estate can be seen in the distance (author's collection)

After a few hundred yards a bridge carries the track over Belmangate (Mark Lloyd)

In 1963 an uncharacteristically clean WD class locomotive number 90339 approaches Belmangate bridge, working an engineer's special from the Loftus direction. Number 90339 was a long-time resident of Wakefield shed at that time so was probably on a local 'running-in' turn after overhaul at Darlington Works, prior to despatch back to its home shed (photo by Harry and Lilian Smith, courtesy of Brian Collins)

Belmangate bridge and the embankment of the Whitby line after closure in the nineteen-sixties, showing what is believed to be an engineer's track-lifting train (photograph by Harry and Lilian Smith, courtesy of John Storey)

An aerial view of Belmangate bridge showing part of the Whitby line. Harry and Lilian Smith's market garden is on the corner plot and allotments cover what is now Eglinton Avenue (Barry Parvin)

Just beyond Belmangate is a three-arch bridge that backs onto Rievaulx Way (Geoff Scurr collection)

(opposite, bottom) By the time this photograph was taken in the mid-nineteen-sixties the line had been abandoned and nature was beginning to take over. This stretch of the line is now completely overgrown with mature trees lining both sides of the track. The three-arch bridge now backs onto Rievaulx Way and the Whitby Lane estate.

During the nineteenth-century a mineral railway from the ironstone mine near the top of Butt Lane ran down the fields and through the middle arch of this bridge, before sweeping west and crossing over Belmangate, via a bridge, in the vicinity of Bank Street and Belmont Terrace. An embankment is still visible near the cricket field.

The derelict brick building in the field to the right of the bridge (opposite, bottom) is believed to be a relic of the long-demolished mineral line. The fields to the left of the picture are now home to the Whitby Lane estate. Rievaulx Way runs parallel to the railway line, merging with it somewhere near the top of the picture. In the distance, at the extreme right, can be seen the grey surface of Butt Lane as it climbs towards Foxdale Farm before turning right and crossing the bridge over the railway line.

*

(below) This three-arch bridge now backs onto gardens on Rievaulx Way. Pam Wilson and her family lived in the house facing the middle arch until the mid-nineteen-eighties.

The three-arch bridge in 1963, six years before the Whitby Lane estate was built (Mark Lloyd)

Butt Lane bridge—a large three-arch construction that spans the railway cutting (Mark Lloyd)

Between Butt Lane and Spawood is a smaller, two-arch bridge (Mark Lloyd)

Further along the Whitby line, in 1963, a North Eastern Railway class Q6, number 63431, negotiates Spawood Viaduct (Ken Taylor collection)

The occasion was an enthusiasts' rail tour on 8 June 1963 with Q6 63431, called the 'Cleveland Limited'. The railway had not been used since 1960 but the line was still passable. Passengers nevertheless had to sign an indemnity before embarking on the tour, in case of any accidents (Ken Taylor collection)

Spawood Viaduct and Fancy Cottage. The track in the foreground came up from Spa ironstone mine, near Waterfall, to merge with the Whitby line in the vicinity of Slapewath (John Linton collection)

Spawood Viaduct still stands but is in disrepair. This magnificent structure is now obscured by trees, invisible to passers by on the adjacent Whitby road—except in winter (John Linton collection)

From Spawood the line approaches Slapewath signal box, with the road from Guisborough to Whitby in the distance. The cottages at Slapewath, still existing, can be seen on the left (John Linton collection)

Fancy Bridge before it was filled in and the Whitby road rerouted (Mark Lloyd)

Compare this postcard of Slapewath to the present road layout—many changes have taken place in this area over the last few decades. The railway was directed behind the houses at Slapewath before continuing onwards to Boosbeck

The rear of Slapewath cottages showing the Whitby line from the road bridge. The Gresley-designed V3 class tank engine 67677, hauling a Guisborough-bound train, was only locally based (at Middlesbrough Newport) for a short period, so this dates the photograph to 1957. Along with many of its class, it was cut up at Darlington Works—in this case in late 1962 (J W Armstrong)

A sad view of Guisborough Station after its abandonment in 1964 (Mark Lloyd)

Guisborough Station during demolition in 1967 (John Linton collection)

The Guisborough Junction signal box stands derelict and vandalised a few years after abandonment (Mark Lloyd)

Rear view of the derelict signal box (Mark Lloyd)

In 1967 Guisborough Station and the Stationmaster's house were demolished. In their place were built the Bow Street Health Centre and a large car park for visitors to the town. It was the end of an era—a sad farewell to over one hundred years of history, and a great loss for the town (John Linton collection)

Demolished at the same time were these cottages on Fountain Street (John Linton collection)

A solitary lamp post stands on the abandoned platform at Guisborough Station (Mark Lloyd)

...and the real last train? An Inspection Special was run from York, on the actual date of closure—2 March 1964—carrying the Chief Civil Engineer to Teesside. The train was headed by B1 class steam locomotive number 61030 *Reedbuck*, arriving from Middlesbrough via Nunthorpe and the Guisborough branch. The presumption is that it continued straight on from Guisborough, travelling along the closed mineral line to Boosbeck, over the badly cracked Spawood viaduct. Its existence was reported in the contemporary railway press. This must have been the last steam locomotive into Guisborough—and the very last train over the line eastwards to Skelton (*Nick Carter*).